Famous Women of the American Revolution

Jeremy Thornton

The Rosen Publishing Group's

PowerKids Press™

New York

For my daughter, Ainsley Sarah

973.3
THO

Published in 2003 by The Rosen Publishing Group, Inc.
29 East 21st Street, New York, NY 10010

First Edition

Editor: Joanne Randolph
Designers: Michael J. Caroleo, Mike Donnellan, Michael de Guzman, Colin Dizengoff

Photo Credits: Cover (left, right), pp. 4, 8, 12, 19 © North Wind Picture Archives; cover (center), p. 15 © courtesy of Independence National Historical Park; back cover, p. 20 (foreground) Library of Congress, Prints and Photographs Division; p. 7 (background) © Hulton/Archive/Getty Images; p. 7 (foreground) courtesy of the Rhode Island Historical Society; p. 11 © Matthew Weber; pp. 16 courtesy of the Massachusetts Historical Society; p. 20 (background) Library of Congress, Manuscript Division.

Manufactured in the United States of America

62610   Famous women of the American Revol

Contents

Revolutionary Women

From 1775 to 1783, the colonies in America fought a war for **independence** from England. We call this war the American Revolution. The Americans had many heroes and famous **patriots** on their side, including George Washington, Paul Revere, and Thomas Jefferson. Yet there were also many female patriots and soldiers. They helped the sick, delivered **supplies**, fought in battles, spied on the British, and helped the American cause in the Revolution in many other ways. Without their help, the colonists might not have won the war.

Molly Pitcher is a legend of the American Revolution. Historians believe that this legend is based on Mary Ludwig Hayes, who helped during the Battle of Monmouth.

Deborah Samson

One woman, Deborah Samson, decided to fight as a soldier. She **disguised** herself as a man and signed up for the army in 1782. She told the other soldiers her name was Robert Shurtliff. She fought for more than a year before anyone found out that she was really a woman. She was a brave soldier who fought well. She was wounded at least twice, once by sword and once by bullet. Finally a doctor found out that she was a woman. She was honorably **discharged** from the army on October 25, 1783. Samson later received a government **pension** for her military service. The state of Massachusetts, where she was born, named her the official **heroine** of the state in 1983.

Deborah Samson was a schoolteacher before she joined the Continental army. After she was discharged, she married Benjamin Gannett and had three children.

Nancy Morgan Hart

Nancy Morgan Hart was another woman who, many believe, helped the colonists. Although there are some different stories about her, it is clear she was a brave woman. During the American Revolution, she spied on the British troops to find out where they were and what they were doing. Her most famous act of **courage** came when six British soldiers entered her house. They told her to feed them. She gave them alcohol to drink while they were waiting for her to cook the food. Then Nancy surprised the soldiers. She grabbed one of their guns, which they had stacked against the wall. One of the soldiers tried to get up, but she shot and killed him. Then she held the others at gunpoint until her neighbors came to help her.

Nancy Morgan Hart was known for being a fierce hunter. She is shown here in this F.O.C. Darley engraving, bravely defending her home against the British soldiers.

Sybil Ludington

On the night of April 26, 1777, a **messenger** came to Sybil Ludington's house. Sybil's father was a colonel in the local **militia**. The messenger told Sybil's family that the British had attacked the town of Danbury, Connecticut. They had taken important supplies of guns and food. The messenger had started to warn the colonists, but he had become too tired to keep riding. Sybil, who was only 16 years old, **volunteered** to warn the colonists. She rode 40 miles (64 km) that night on her horse, Star. She told the colonists of the British attack. The colonial soldiers gathered to fight the British and marched to Danbury. As a result of Sybil's courage, the colonists drove the British soldiers out of Danbury and saved the supplies.

This statue of Sybil Ludington was sculpted in 1960 by Anna Huntington. The statue, which celebrates Sybil's brave ride of April 26, 1777, is in Carmel, New York.

SYBIL LUDINGTON
REVOLUTIONARY WAR HEROINE
APRIL 26, 1777
CALLED OUT THE VOLUNTEER MILITIA, BY RIDING
THROUGH THE NIGHT, ALONE ON HORSEBACK, AT
THE AGE OF 16, ALERTING THE COUNTRYSIDE TO
THE BURNING OF DANBURY, CONN. BY THE BRITISH
PLACED BY
ENOCH CROSBY CHAPTER
D.A.R.
PRESENTED BY
ANNA HYATT HUNTINGTON
1961

PHILLIS WHEATLEY, NEGRO SERVANT to Mr. JOHN WHEATLEY, of BOSTON.

Phillis Wheatley

Phillis Wheatley was the first African American writer to have a book **published**. She was born in 1753 and started writing poetry when she was about 13 years old. She wrote about many things. Some of her poetry showed her **support** of the American Revolution and inspired people to fight for the patriotic cause. In one poem, she compared the British king's control of America with a slave owner's control of his slaves. She wrote one piece about an 11-year-old boy, Christopher Snyder, who was killed in an **incident** between the colonists and the British. She also wrote a poem about the Boston Massacre, which happened very close to where she lived. After an amazing and inspiring life, she died of poor health in 1784.

This picture was in Wheatley's first book of poems, *Poems* on *Various Subjects*, *Religious* and *Moral*, published in 1773. Wheatley was freed from slavery that year.

Martha Washington

Martha Washington also supported the American Revolution. She was the wife of George Washington, the commander in chief of the Continental army. That gave her a lot of responsibility. She had to be brave and to support the cause. Martha stayed with him in army camps every winter. In March 1777, George was ill, and Martha stayed with him and nursed him back to health. She used her free time to help the soldiers. She also used her influence to inspire other women to help. She and the wives of the other officers sewed clothes for the soldiers to wear on the battlefield. They also helped to care for the sick and the wounded.

Martha Washington was born on June 2, 1731, in Virginia. Though she liked living quietly, she supported her husband as he became the leader of a new nation.

Abigail Adams

Abigail Adams was another woman who used her position in society to support the American cause. Her husband, John Adams, was an important American patriot. He served in the Continental Congress and later became president of the United States. He often asked Abigail for advice. She wrote letters to her husband and to her friends, supporting the colonists in the American Revolution. She also thought women should have a voice in the new U.S. government. John shared some of her letters with the men in Congress. He wanted them to know how the Revolution was affecting the colonists at home. Abigail's letters and advice played an important role in the creation of the new nation.

Abigail Adams, shown here in a 1766 portrait by Benjamin Blyth, managed the farm and raised a family while her husband was helping to found the new nation.

Mercy Otis Warren

Mercy Otis Warren was a popular writer who helped the Americans in the American Revolution. She used her writings to **encourage** the colonists during the war. She wrote poems, plays, and **satires**. Her works often made fun of the British. She published her works without signing her name so that the British would not be able to put her in jail. Several important patriots, including George Washington and John Adams, often met at her house to talk about the war. She was also a close friend of Abigail Adams's. She **corresponded** with these important people through letters. Through her writings, her thoughts and ideas about independence and democracy influenced many American patriots.

Mercy Otis Warren, pictured here in this portrait based on a 1763 John Singleton Copley painting, played an important part in shaping American ideas.

The Maryland Journal, and Baltimore Advertiser.

[Vol. VI.]   TUESDAY, July 6, 1779.   [Numb. 302.]

PENNSYLVANIA (PHILADELPHIA) —, 1779.

Some QUERIES, *political and military; humbly offered to the consideration of the* PUBLIC.

I. WHETHER George the First did not, on his accession to the Throne of Great-Britain, by making himself King of a party, instead of the whole nation, sow the seeds not only of the subversion of the liberties of the People, but of the ruin of the whole empire?

II. Whether, by proscribing that class of men to which his Ministry were pleased to give the appellation of Tories, he did not, in the end, make them not only real Tories, but even Jacobites?

III. Whether the consequence of this distinction, now be———— was not ———— rebellions—and whether the fruit of ———————, not septennial Par————, a large ———— an enormous additional weight ———— into the scale of the Crown, ———— down not only the substance, ———— sense of patriotism, the mo———— turned the mighty fa————

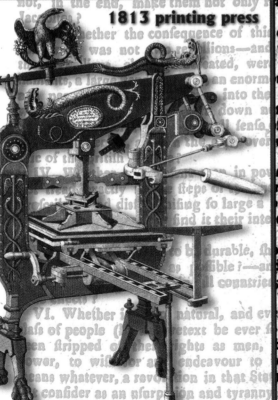

1813 printing press

IV. Whether ———— in power, in this State, do ———— steps of ———— pernicious Ministry, by ———— disfranchising so large a proportion of citizens ———— find it their interest to brand with the ————

———— be durable, should not be constructed ———— plausible?—and whether the same ———— all countries, do not produce the ————

VI. Whether it be natural, and even justifiable, for that class of people (————text be ever so plausible) who have been stripped of their rights as men, by the hard hand of power, to wish for and endeavour to bring about, by any means whatever, a revolution in that State, which they cannot consider as an usurpation and tyranny?

VII. Whether a subject of Morocco be not (when we con————human nature) a step less mortal than a disfranchised citizen———— Pennsylvania—as ———— former has the comfort of seeing

valuable country? Did it prevent the enemy's ships from passing or repassing, with impunity.

XVIII. Whether, when General Howe manifestly gave over all thoughts of attacking General Washington, in the last strong position in the rear of White-Plains, and fell back towards York-Island, orders should not have been immediately despatched for the evacuation of Fort-Washington, and for the removal of all the stores of value from Fort Lee to some secure spot, more removed from the river?—Whether this was not proposed, and the proposal slighted?

XIX. Whether the loss of the garrison of Fort-Washington, and its consequent loss of Fort-Lee, with the tents, stores, &c. had not such an effect on the spirits of the people, as to make the difference of twenty thousand men to America?

XX. Whether, in the defeat of Brandewine, General Sullivan was really the person who ought to have been censured?

XXI. * Whether, if Duke Ferdinand had commanded at German-Town, after having gained, by the valour of his troops, and the negligence of his enemy, a partial victory, he would have contrived, by a single stroke of the Bathos, to have corrupted this partial victory into a defeat?

XXII. Whether our position at Valley-Forge was not such, that if General Howe, or afterwards General Clinton, had been well informed of its circumstances, defects, and vices, they might not, at the head of ten, or even of eight, thousand men, have reduced the American army to the same fatal necessity as the Americans did General Burgoyne?

XXIII. Whether the trials of General St. Clair, of which Court-Martial General Lincoln was President, and that on General Lee, were conducted in the same forms, and on the same principles?—Whether, in the former, all hearsay evidences were not absolutely rejected; and, in the latter, hearsay evidence did not constitute a very considerable part?

XXIV. Whether, if the Generals Schuyler and St. Clair had been tried by the same Court-Martial as General Lee was, and, instead of Congress, General Washington had been the prosecutor, those Gentlemen (unexceptionable as their conduct was) would not have stood a very ugly chance of being condemned? And he, ———— if instead of General Washington, Congress ————

Mary Katherine Goddard

Mary Katherine Goddard was another important woman who used publishing to help the Americans during the American Revolution. She and her brother, William, published the *Providence Gazette*, which was the first newspaper in Providence, Rhode Island. In 1773, they moved to Baltimore, Maryland. There they started the *Maryland Journal*, the first newspaper in that city. During the war, Goddard published many newspaper articles supporting American independence. She also published stories about the battles. In 1777, she published the first copy of the Declaration of Independence, which included the names of the signers. From 1775 to 1789, Goddard served as the **postmaster** of Baltimore.

This is the July 6, 1779, issue of Goddard's *Maryland Journal, and Baltimore Advertiser*. This article is about the political and military issues of that time.

Women at Home
and in the Camps

In addition to these heroines, there were many more women who made it possible for the war to carry on. Many women stayed at home and took care of the farms or the businesses while the men were fighting for freedom from Britain. They continued to raise their families and to take care of their homes. Some women traveled with the armies. They helped the men by cooking their food and by washing their clothes. They cared for the sick and the wounded. They carried food and supplies to those on the battlefield and to those taken prisoner by the British. Some women even made bullets for use in the war. Women of all ages and backgrounds played an important part in making the United States the country it is today.

Glossary

corresponded (kor-ih-SPOND-ed) Communicated with other people, often through letters.

courage (KUR-ij) Bravery.

discharged (dis-CHARJD) Released from military duty.

disguised (dis-GYZD) Wore a costume or an outfit to hide one's identity.

encourage (in-KUR-uj) To inspire with confidence.

heroine (HER-uh-wuhn) A woman who is admired for her qualities or deeds.

incident (IN-sih-dent) Something that happens.

independence (in-dih-PEN-dents) Freedom from the control of other people.

messenger (MEH-sin-jur) A person who delivers information or news.

militia (muh-LIH-shuh) A group of people who are trained and ready to fight in an emergency.

patriots (PAY-tree-uhts) People who love and defend their country.

pension (PEN-shun) Periodic payments to a person who has retired.

postmaster (POST-mas-ter) One who is in charge of the post office.

published (PUH-blishd) Printed for distribution to the public.

satires (SA-tyrz) Literary pieces that make fun of actions or ideas; often of the government.

supplies (suh-PLYZ) Provisions of food, ammunition, or other necessary items.

support (suh-PORT) To uphold or help someone.

volunteered (vah-luhn-TEERD) Offered to do something without being paid.

Index

Primary Sources

Cover and page 7: This portrait of Deborah Samson is held at the Rhode Island Historical Society. It was created around 1797. Accession # 1900.6.1 **Page 8:** This is a hand-colored engraving by F.O.C. Darley who lived from 1821 to 1888. The engraving is held at the New York Public Library in their print collection. **Page 12:** This is a hand-colored woodcut of Phillis Wheatley. It was first published by Archer Bell in 1773. Copies of the print are held by the Massachusetts Historical Society, the National Portrait Gallery, the Library of Congress, the New York Public Library, and the University of North Carolina at Chapel Hill Libraries. **Cover and page 15:** This is an oil painting of Martha Washington by Charles Willson Peale from 1795. It is part of the collection of the Independence National Historic Park. **Page 16:** This 1766 oil painting by Benjamin Blyth is held at the Massachusetts Historical Society. Blyth greatly admired Abigail's features and said that painting Abigail Adams was much more interesting than painting her husband. **Page 19:** The hand-colored engraving of Mercy Otis Warren is based on a 1763 oil painting by John Singleton Copley. The original is held in the collections at the Museum of Fine Arts in Boston. It was donated at the bequest of Winslow Warren in 1931. **Page 20:** This is a section of the July 6, 1779, issue of Mary Katherine Goddard's *Maryland Journal, and Baltimore Advertiser*. This particular article discusses political and military issues of that time. On top of the article is an 1813 engraving of a printing press drawn by William Strickland and engraved by Hugh Anderson. His engraving, which appeared in Abraham Rees's *The Cyclopedia*, shows what kind of press was probably used to print Goddard's newspaper.

Web Sites

Due to the changing nature of Internet links, PowerKids Press has developed an online list of Web sites related to the subject of this book. This site is updated regularly. Please use this link to access the list:

www.powerkidslinks.com/bad/famwom/